Stamford, Bourne and the Deepings

— Landscapes and Legends —

Text by Rex Needle
Paintings by Alan Oliver

First published by Cottage Publications,
an imprint of Laurel Cottage Ltd.
Donaghadee, N. Ireland 2009

Design & origination in Northern Ireland.
Printed & bound in China.
ISBN 978 1 900935 76 0

The Author

Rex Needle is a retired journalist having worked in the old Fleet Street, now long gone, and later in the provinces as a freelance for the national, provincial and overseas press, and as a broadcaster for the BBC for 20 years. He has lived in Bourne since 1983 and is now the local historian, writing several books and numerous articles on the subject and is the author of the definitive history of the town, *A Portrait of Bourne* (on CD-ROM), containing a staggering 1½ million words of text and 4,000 photographs, both historic and contemporary, copies of which are now in the public libraries and Lincolnshire County Archives.

Now 78, he continues writing and editing the Bourne web site, Bourne in Words and Pictures, launched in 1998 and now probably the longest running community web site for a town of this size, winning several awards and attracting more than 2,000 visitors a week from around the world. He has been married to Elke for almost 50 years and she is his invaluable help, proof-reading every word written and advising on pictures and presentation.

The Artist

Alan Oliver is recognised as one of the leading landscape artists in the Midlands. He was born in Southampton but his family moved to Stamford when he was three and his first job was as an engineering apprentice with Baker Perkins at Peterborough.

He later became a graphic designer and technical illustrator before working as a film animator and eventually becoming a professional artist. His distinctive work has popularised the beauty of many English counties, as his work in this volume demonstrates. Alan lives in Oakham and although now 71, remains in great demand for commissions and exhibitions.

Contents

An Introduction

The segment of countryside in South Lincolnshire which embraces Stamford, Bourne and the Deepings retains much of its old world charm although change is coming, albeit slowly, with the onward encroachment of tarmac, bricks and mortar as new roads are built and housing estates appear, boosting once modest populations.

Although they share the same topographical identification, all being within the jurisdiction of that district known as South Kesteven, they are diversely different in appearance, Stamford being universally recognised for its mellow stone buildings amid an undulating countryside while Bourne sits between uplands and fen and is predominantly red brick with the cottages and farmsteads of the Deepings beyond amid a landscape of wide open skies.

Yet they are inextricably linked, each having an aspect of life past or present which identifies one with another, thus creating a familiar atmosphere by which the inhabitants of one place may feel equally at home in another. Those in Bourne may work in Stamford, those in the Deepings may shop in Bourne and so on, for that which one centre lacks may be provided by the other but all are separated by short drives through attractive countryside interspersed by interesting villages, making it a rewarding occupation for anyone with time to spare, to stop and stare, to turn off the main highways and see for themselves, because they will find mills and manors, churches and coaching inns, old cottages and houses, dykes and rivers bordered by ancient woodlands, for this area is the nearest you will get to finding an unwrecked England.

PUBLIC LIBRARY
TOILETS
Alan Oliver

Stamford

Stamford has a reputation as the finest stone town in England and few can fail to be enchanted by its splendid buildings, old churches, quaint and narrow cobbled streets and connecting passageways, all of which are redolent of times past. It is richly fashioned and mellowed, as indeed it was 300 years ago because in 1697, the traveller Celia Fiennes described it *'as fine a built town all of stone as may be seen'* and there are few who would disagree today.

In the early days, the town was at the very heart of Roman Britain, famous for its pottery, wool and woollen cloth. In Danish times it was the selected capital of the fens and one of the Five Boroughs of the Danelaw. Mediaeval Stamford was also known throughout Europe as a centre for religious learning and many of its monastic buildings remain.

A charter was granted by Henry III in 1254 with the start of ecclesiastical building, although great damage was done during the Wars of the Roses and in 1461 a Lancastrian army burned much of it to the ground, but revival came with the construction of the Welland Navigation canal bringing with it new industries creating a source of wealth that renewed the town's livelihood and so the present day Stamford gradually began to emerge.

It was initially a walled town but only a small proportion of the wall now remains although its overall appearance has survived relatively unspoiled, a jewel in our country's architectural landscape within the original mediaeval pattern that remains and is essentially the same oval area of 1,000 yards by 400 yards.

There was a castle here, first noted in the Domesday Book of 1086, and its construction was probably part of a concerted policy of defensive building by William I during his conquest of the north in the early years of his reign. The site was a small hill overlooking the River Welland but the mound was levelled in 1935 to provide a car park, now the bus station. Rubble outhouses at the corner of Castle Dyke and Bath Row with three arches from the 14th century are all that remain of the castle buildings and a postern gate from the same period also stands in Bath Row together with a short section of wall.

Stamford is particularly renowned for its fine collection of churches, more than any other town of its size in England and they are the tallest buildings in the town. The 13th century tower of St. Mary's for instance, is topped with a soaring broach spire 163 feet high that was added a hundred years later. All Saints, which dominates Red Lion Square, has a great perpendicular style tower and spire with most of the work inside dating from the 13th century. St. George's is smaller and more intimate than the others while the late 15th century St. John's and St. Martin's are also most interesting buildings, the latter containing a magnificent renaissance monument to William Cecil, the first Lord Burghley, the illustrious English statesman who was Lord High Treasurer and trusted chief adviser to Queen Elizabeth I and who built Burghley House as his country home and estate. He died in 1598 and his effigy lies upon a table tomb in armour and garter robes with the staff of office in his hands.

His descendants were created Earls of Exeter in 1605 and Marquesses of Exeter in 1801, all of whom lived at Burghley House. One of them was the 6th Marquess of Exeter, David George Brownlow Cecil (1905-1981), styled Lord Burghley before 1956 and also known as David Burghley who distinguished himself as an English athlete, sports official and Conservative politician, winning a gold medal in the 400 metres hurdles at the 1928 Summer Olympics in Amsterdam.

There is a civic pride in the appearance of Stamford which has more than 600 buildings listed as being of architectural or historical importance, these constituting half of those in the whole of Lincolnshire. Today, the town has a modest population of around 20,000 and a market town atmosphere with intimate shops dealing with antiques and crafts, fashion and furniture and, of course, rural pursuits, because this is also the home of the Burghley Horse Trials, held here annually since 1961. It was therefore no surprise when in October 1967, the town gained the distinction of being the first in England to be designated a Conservation Area under the Civic Administration Act and its ancient character now attracts many film makers who have discovered that these historic streets are excellent as locations for a variety of period drama productions that are screened worldwide.

During the 18th century, the streets were the scene of an annual ritual known as bull running, an event which was eventually banned by law because of its cruelty. According to tradition, the custom dated from the time of King John but fell into disuse until 1756 when a mayor of the town left a sum of money to revive the practice every year on November 13th. The ritual began shortly before 11am when the bell of St. Mary's church tolled and the streets were blocked at each end by carts and wagons as the bull was turned loose. The animal was then provoked by missiles, shouting and sharp sticks and once it started to run, the barricades were removed and the entire gathering of bull, men, boys and dogs rushed helter skelter through the streets, the objective being to steer it towards the bridge over the river where it was seized and thrown over the parapet into the water, eventually being slaughtered and its flesh sold off cheaply to enable the merrymakers to finish off the day with a beef supper.

The custom was met by disapproval in many quarters and the first attempt to end it came in 1788 when a town proclamation was issued stating that it was contrary to religion, law, and nature, and punishable with the penalty of death, but this had little effect. In the following years, troops and police were sent in but they too failed to halt the practice and it was not until 1839 that bull running was finally abolished after several confrontations with officers from the Society for Prevention of Cruelty to Animals (later to become the RSPCA) and the intervention of the Home Secretary.

The Great North Road or A1 once ran through the very centre of this historic town causing many problems for its inhabitants and for its old buildings which by the mid-20th century were beginning to show signs of damage from fumes and vibration. A concerted campaign by the public and the local authorities persuaded government that such a situation could not continue and in 1962 the long-awaited bypass was completed, so ending those years of inconvenience as the streams of heavy vehicles were suddenly halted.

The town's scholastic tradition began in the 14th century when during 1333-34 a group of tutors and students from Brasenose Hall, Oxford, became dissatisfied with conditions at their university and migrated to Stamford although the breakaway university was short-lived because the rebellious students were ordered to return to Oxford by Edward III. Only the gateway of their new Brasenose College still exists, standing isolated in St. Paul's Street on the southern entrance to the town, although the ornate knocker which once adorned the front has been replaced by a replica.

Today, there is still a touch of town and gown in Stamford for this is home to one of the country's leading public schools. Stamford School was founded in 1532 with a main frontage on St. Paul's Street while at the other end of the town in St. Martin's is Stamford High School, a public school for girls founded in 1876. Pupils from both can be seen most days during term time in their distinctive uniforms, either striding out between lessons in the various classrooms or off to call at the shops in the town centre which is now largely a pedestrianised precinct with a mosaic of yellow paving blocks underfoot.

Many former pupils of Stamford School have made their mark in life, notably Sir Malcolm Sargent, conductor and darling of the Promenade Concerts at the Albert Hall in London. He died in 1967, aged 72, and is buried in the town cemetery where his marble cross is inscribed *'Promenader's Prayer'*. Others include the composer Sir Michael Tippett and the writer Colin Dexter, author of the Inspector Morse series, dramatised by television. General Sir Mike Jackson (born 1944) was also a pupil, serving in the school's army cadet force before going on to a distinguished military career and eventually becoming Chief of the General Staff.

The gateway to the new Brasenose College

The schools make a large contribution to the prosperity of Stamford which also has a major employer in the Royal Air Force base at nearby Wittering, home of the Harrier jump jet, while local industries specialise in engineering and the production of cement which uses limestone quarried on site at nearby Ketton. The *Stamford Mercury* has been published here since 1695 making it Britain's oldest newspaper.

The public library is a handsome building erected in 1804 and designed in the classical style with a magnificent Tuscan portico. It was once used as a meat market but converted for its present role a century later and now looks very smart and attractive in the early morning sunshine because the ancient stonework has recently been cleaned.

In the churchyard at St. Martin's is the grave of Daniel Lambert who achieved fame as England's fattest man. He lived in Leicester and died in 1809 at the age of 39 while visiting Stamford for a day at the races, a popular sport at that time although the racecourse closed in 1874. He was 5 feet 11 inches tall, had a 92-inch waist, measured 37 inches round the leg, weighed almost 53 stones and is remembered by a tombstone erected by his friends while some of his clothing is on display in the town's museum.

The Stamford Shakespeare Company is one of the main cultural features in the region, attracting thousands each year to nearby Tolethorpe Hall, one of Europe's finest open air theatres. Since 1977 productions of the bard's work have been presented each summer in this beautiful location with enchanting sets and gorgeous costumes that never fail to thrill the theatre goer, accompanied by a picnic on the lawn or a meal in the restaurant.

Such a rich heritage attracts thousands of visitors each year and this has created a thriving tourist trade offering a wide range of accommodation, from the traditional bed and breakfast to hotels, houses and flats for weekly and weekend lets. Many farmers in the surrounding villages have diversified by turning disused stables and outbuildings into holiday cottages to take advantage of this growing industry. The local tourist association is always ready to help with a busy information centre that also offers a series of leaflets detailing the various town trails pointing visitors to the best routes that take in the most interesting places.

One thing is certain for those who visit: you will most definitely return. No place, especially an old town such as this, reveals all of its fascinating features during one visit and this is particularly true of Stamford.

The road which runs into Stamford from the north is known as High Street St. Martin's which until 1962 was also the Great North Road, haunt of highwaymen in past times. The gallows beam that can still be seen spanning the road was erected as a sign of welcome to the honest traveller and as a warning to gentlemen of the road such as Tom King and Dick Turpin of the fate that awaited them if caught practising their trade in the vicinity.

The highway has been famous for centuries and there has always been an inn by the River Welland which the road crosses at this point, giving food and shelter to hungry and weary travellers. The exact age of the George Hotel is not known but as historians believe that it was once owned by the Abbots of Croyland (now Crowland), then it has probably been in business for over a thousand years. It would have been comparatively small in those days, encompassing two religious houses, one of them the Holy Sepulchre, a hospital of the Knights of St. John of Jerusalem who accompanied pilgrims on their journeys.

It has been progressively enlarged with the passing of the years. Always a hostelry of great renown and frequented by nobility and royalty, King Charles I stayed there on two occasions and Sir Walter Scott, the Scottish historical novelist and poet, often visited and it was he who wrote that the view of Stamford from St. Martins was *'the finest twixt Edinburgh and London'.* During the 18th and 19th centuries, forty stage coaches a day passed through between London and York when the time allowed for the mail coach from Stamford to reach the capital was nine hours and 20 minutes, including a change of horses en route.

The inn is steeped in history but restored and maintained over the years with great care and sympathy to make certain that its ancient features are not destroyed, thus ensuring that it remains an outstanding example of old England, and a luxurious one at that.

The George Hotel

STAMFORD

THE GEORGE
THE GEORGE OF STAMFORD
Alan Oliver.

A Benedictine monastery known as St. Leonard's Priory and founded between 1080 and 1140 was amongst the earliest of Stamford's religious buildings and can still be seen on the outskirts of the town. This is just one of a group of religious establishments that appeared in mediaeval times, others being the Nunnery of St. Mary which was established at Wothorpe in 1109, St. Michael's Priory at Little Wothorpe in 1150, Blackfriars circa 1222, Whitefriars (1260), Greyfriars (1266) and the Austin Friars which were founded in 1380.

The extensive remains of St. Leonard's can be found isolated in a field off Priory Road to the east of the town, well off the tourist track yet steeped in history and built on the site of an earlier foundation. Tradition suggests that it may have been the work of St. Wilfred (634-709), English bishop and saint, who also built the 7th century crypts at Hexham Priory and Ripon Cathedral.

Wilfred was a controversial figure in the church, his life coinciding with those of Cuthbert and Benedict Biscop, all of whom helped to convert the Anglo-Saxon kingdoms of England to Christianity. During one of his spells of exile he served as Bishop at Leicester before his death at Oundle at the age of 75. It is believed that he built the priory in 658 on land given by Alcnfrid, son of King Oswy of Northumbria, but this is uncertain, although it may well be the most ancient religious house in Lincolnshire.

The present building is part of the nave of the church, dating from the early 12th century and recent excavations indicate that there were extensive buildings on the site. What survives is the north arcade and part of the impressive west front of the church which was constructed about 1150, just before Gothic became the dominant force in ecclesiastical architecture. Edward I is known to have stayed here when passing through the town and it has many other historic connections although its tourist potential has not been exploited in recent years, perhaps because of its out of the way location, but it is still worth a visit.

St. Leonard's Priory

STAMFORD

Alan Oliver.

One of the most unusual of Stamford's churches is St. Michael's, also known as St. Michael the Greater, which stands in the High Street pedestrian precinct surrounded by shops but then that is exactly what this building is now, having been converted for commercial use.

There is evidence that there was a church on this spot in 1158 but the building was extensively altered at least twice in later centuries while the east end was rebuilt in 1707 with a wooden tower. This caused some interest later in the century when a humorous poem about it was published in *The Gentleman's Magazine* in April 1761 suggesting that a church with a tower made of wood *'can produce nothing good'* and it was eventually replaced with one made of stone.

The Rev Charles Swann became rector in the summer of 1831 and arranged for new pews to be installed but the following year when attempts were made to improve the church interior through the removal of alternate pillars, the building collapsed on 8th June 1832. Materials salvaged from the ruins included 20 tons of lead and oak beams which were sold for scrap and in 1835 work began on building the present church in the Early English style at a cost of £2,800. The re-consecration was carried out in October 1836 at a service attended by the Bishop of Lincoln and seventy members of the clergy.

In 1962, the church was closed due to a population shift away from the town centre and remained unused for twenty years during which time vandals broke in and destroyed many of the remaining fittings. Then in 1981, after several years of controversy over the best use for the property (conversion into an old people's home and an arts centre being among the suggestions discussed), the church was sold for redevelopment as a shopping arcade and is now back in use as one of the most distinctive buildings in the High Street, housing two shops, a building society and an insurance company in the tower while the adjoining graveyard has been turned into an open space with public seats.

St. Michael's Church

STAMFORD

HEALTH BEAUTY
Alan Oliver

A green swathe of pastureland lying alongside the banks of the River Welland is one of the delights of this ancient town and The Meadows has been a place of leisure and recreation for centuries.

This is common land divided by the Enclosure Act of 1871, bordered by the Mill Stream on one side and the River Welland on the other, and is three fields long, the first being the responsibility of the town council and the next two belonging to the freemen. It is here that the townspeople and visitors exercise or take their dogs for a stroll as well as being the scene of holiday events and celebratory gatherings such as music festivals and antique fairs.

Nearby is the stone Stamford Spa, a mineral iron water spring once much sought after for its medicinal properties. The well was first used in 1819 and was extremely fast flowing and frequently used by those who were ill and seeking out its soothing influence, reckoned to have been induced by the iron oxide, carbonate of lime and sulphate of lime which it contained. In fact, it became so popular and well used that in 1864 a stone coping was placed over the outlet on the orders of the mayor, John Paradise, to improve its unsightly appearance.

Once known as the water meadows, this pleasant spot is also the perfect place to picnic on a sunny day, to watch or feed the waterfowl while also providing walking routes along the river, all mapped out at varying distances by the town council to cater for young and old, the energetic and the less vigorous. The paths also take in many features along the way, notably a stone pillar at the site of the old Roman ford known as the Boudicca Monument which records the pursuit of the remnants of the Ninth Legion by the Queen of the Iceni people of Eastern England who led a major uprising against the occupying Roman forces in AD 61. It is also the starting point for the Jurassic Way and there are footpaths leading to neighbouring villages.

The Meadows

STAMFORD

Alan Oliver

The stately home built by William Cecil, the first Lord Burghley, is now a major tourist attraction for Stamford, the largest and grandest house of the first Elizabethan age whose impressive 'Bottle Lodges' entrance gates signal the delights that await within. Burghley House was built on the site of a 12th century monastery and took 32 years to complete between 1565 and 1587 and William Cecil appears to have been his own architect.

The house contains over 240 rooms and the interior was extensively altered in the late 17th century by John, the 5th Earl of Exeter, a devoted connoisseur of fine art who established the immense collections that can be seen on show today. Capability Brown made architectural alterations and additions in the late 18th century, landscaping the gardens and deer park and constructing the beautiful lake with its Lion Bridge, the stable courtyard and the Orangery.

Hermann Goering, a leading member of the Nazi Party who lived in Rutland while studying in England during the early 20th century, visited the house several times and vowed that it would be his home following a successful invasion of England during the Second World War. Today, it remains a family home for William Cecil's descendants, centre of an agricultural estate of some 10,000 acres and attracting thousands of visitors each year who come to see the eighteen magnificent staterooms crammed with paintings, Chinese and Japanese porcelain, furniture, tapestries and textiles and intricate wood carvings by Grinling Gibbons. A guided tour takes them through the splendid interiors with a panorama of the grounds and parkland through the windows.

The oldest part of the house is the Great Hall, a room 60 feet long by 65 feet high which has a splendid hammer beam roof and contains one of the world's largest silver wine coolers. Many of the rooms have painted ceilings – the Heaven Room by Antonio Verrio completed in 1694 being regarded as the most memorable in the house, a masterpiece of illusionistic frescoes depicting cavorting classical Gods and demigods, a triumph of perspective painting considered to be the finest painted room in England.

Burghley House

STAMFORD

Alan Oliver

The theatrical tradition in Stamford is long and distinguished and is perpetuated by the old theatre in St. Mary's Street dating back two and a half centuries. It opened in 1768 and flourished over the next 100 years with many of the famous names from the English stage appearing here to thrill audiences including Edmund Keane, often regarded as the greatest ever English actor, and other leading thespians.

But its popularity as a stage venue declined and as the visits of touring companies became less frequent, the building was converted into a gentleman's club and remained so until the Second World War when it became a rendezvous for servicemen and women serving at the nearby camps or home on leave. When the war ended, the building was used for a variety of purposes including badminton, flower shows, jumble sales, discos and even dog training.

The Marquess of Exeter then made the building available to a dedicated group of enthusiasts who set about a programme of refurbishment and it re-opened in 1976 for modern day performances and so it remains one of the few 18th century theatres in Britain still serving its original purpose. Today the restored Georgian theatre seats 166 people and has been refurbished to extremely high modern standards. As a reminder of its eminent past, a door believed to be one of the original stage doors can still be seen in the theatre foyer. Apart from theatrical presentations, it also doubles up as a modern cinema which opened in 1994, created when a wide screen is lowered across the width of the stage and the latest sound system is plugged in.

The ballroom which survives next door was originally the Stamford Assembly Rooms, used for concerts and social functions since 1727 and restored in 1972. The buildings now form the arts centre complex and offer between them a wealth of entertainment drawn from the very best national and international touring drama, music, dance, comedy and exhibition while also providing a wide range of additional facilities for the community including various function rooms and the town's Tourist Information Centre.

Stamford Theatre

STAMFORD

STAMFORD
THEATRE
Alan Oliver

One of the finest and best preserved buildings is Browne's Hospital in Broad Street. It was endowed in 1475 during the reign of Edward IV by a rich and influential wool merchant William Browne and was called the Hospital of All Saints.

Browne and his brother John were also largely responsible for enlarging and embellishing the Church of All Saints which is nearby and he was elected an alderman of Stamford six times between 1435 and 1470 and three times Sheriff of Rutland before he died in 1489. He and his wife and family are believed to have lived in a house on the western side of the hospital and would have been parishioners of All Saints where brasses relating to three generations of the family may be seen. The hospital, or bedehouse, required inmates to attend chapel twice a day when masses were said for the souls of the founders but on Sundays they worshipped at All Saints.

This is one of England's outstanding mediaeval almshouses, built for ten poor men and two women and managed by a warden and chaplain. Originally consisting of a common room on the ground floor divided into cubicles and the layout can still be seen today because it is marked in wood on the floor. Above was the Audit Room and a chapel with other offices arranged around a courtyard. The entire building was enlarged in 1870, separate cottages being built for the inmates together with a new house for the warden. Further extensive modernisation took place in 1963 when the cottages were upgraded into flats, each with a living room, bedroom, kitchen and bathroom.

A Tudor screen in excellent condition remains in the little chapel that was consecrated in 1494 and still has its original pews and a pre-Reformation altar slab. There is much stained glass of considerable beauty, restored by the Pilgrim Trust in 1964. Today, the hospital is a registered charity, managed by a board of governors and trustees, remaining in public use and featuring a museum of almshouse life which is open to visitors during the summer months.

Browne's Hospital
Stamford

Alan Oliver

Local government has been administered and justice dispensed from the Town Hall in St. Mary's Street for more than two centuries and it is a stately reminder of the architectural grandeur of Stamford as you drive in from the south up St. Mary's Hill with the imposing tower and spire of the church ahead. It was built in 1777 as home to the corporation, now the town council, while it also served as a magistrates court until recent years. Inside can also be found the town regalia, a collection of silver emblems and artefacts that are reckoned to be the finest of any town of this size in England.

The history of the corporation can be traced back to the reign of Edward the Confessor in the 11th century when the town was governed by twelve lawmen or magistrates, the style of alderman being introduced in the 14th century. In 1461, a charter from Edward IV conferred many privileges on the Alderman and Burgesses of Stamford enabling the town to manage its own affairs free from the jurisdiction of the sheriff. The minute book of the corporation commencing in 1461 is preserved in the Town Hall and the silver mace also dates from this time.

New charters were granted by Charles II in 1663 and the title of chief magistrate was changed from alderman to mayor. Until the establishment of our county police forces in 1839, the corporation kept a Town Watch of six men for night duty and twelve burgesses were chosen each year by the magistrates to act as constables. A beadle was also appointed and, provided with a resplendent uniform, he also attended upon the mayor and acted as a constable.

In 1974, the re-organisation of local government brought a complete end to the old order when the office of alderman was abolished, Stamford lost its borough status and its powers were swallowed up by newly-formed county and district councils but it retained a town council with the authority to elect a chairman or mayor each year. It is this council which retains the link with the past by continuing to meet at the Town Hall.

STAMFORD

Alan Oliver

Stamford originally grew from a Danish settlement at the lowest point that the River Welland could be crossed by ford or bridge and was the only one of the five Danelaw boroughs not to become a county town. The ford existed on the Roman road known as Ermine Street where it passed through the town and this remains the only crossing for traffic which now uses the town bridge between St. Mary's Hill and High Street St. Martins. It was built of stone in 1849 with a generous span of three arches and designed by the distinguished ecclesiastical architect, Edward Browning, who was responsible for many other buildings in the locality and is best remembered for his work on churches and chapels.

The demanding use of this one crossing for traffic in and out of Stamford to and from the north remains a local transport anxiety and although there have been successive proposals there are no immediate plans to improve it. The result is that all traffic using the roads within the area of the bridge are controlled by traffic lights and there are often delays although none are quite as bad as those experienced by the town when the bridge also formed part of the Great North Road or A1, now thankfully diverted on to the bypass.

The bridge remains a remarkable reminder of the Victorian age, its golden stone enhancing the view of the river from the Meadows and attracting photographers and artists wishing to capture the mellow richness of its colours, especially at sunset. Around the bridge, developers have lost no opportunity in using the riverbank wherever possible to build high quality housing to take advantage of the river view and so blocks of flats have sprung up to fill the unsightly gaps of past years. The standard of the new build properties within sight of the river is a reminder that this is the very heart of the town's conservation area and the work of those from years past who fought to retain its heritage and ensure that the protection they introduced would remain for future generations.

The River Bridge

STAMFORD

Alan Oliver

The beauty of Stamford is best seen by those who explore on foot because the town is revealed as a maze of narrow streets and alleyways all lined with historic buildings, timber-framed and stone houses from centuries past, although many of those in the town centre are now converted for commercial use.

St. Mary's Street, for instance, has become a busy shopping centre selling a wide range of goods including antiques, leather and fine quality porcelain, while still dominated by the imposing tower and spire of St. Mary's, a church whose origins date back to 1146. This is one of the many Anglican churches in the town and, although not the oldest, it is generally regarded as the mother church, a tradition that stems from the close connection with the borough corporation because it once housed the former guild from which it sprang and there is evidence that it was used for civic functions in the past.

As with most of the town's other churches, their name is used in many of the neighbouring streets which is evident here, particularly St. Mary's Place, a short and quaint side road around the church which connects with St. Mary's Hill. Now used mainly for car parking, St. Mary's Place is paved with cobblestones reflecting the appearance of the town of yesteryear when prosperous professional men and merchants were attracted to live here, building their fine vernacular and later classical or Georgian houses which today provide the greater part of the town's fabric.

There is also a secluded section of St. Mary's Street, away from the main road, again flanked by historic stone buildings, the grandest of which is the sombre, colonnaded Stamford Hotel dating from 1829 with the Statue of Justice by J C F Rossi, RA at its summit and possessing one of the longest Regency frontages in the county. The building is now converted into shops known as Stamford Walk while nearby, No 40 St. Martin's Street dates back to 1500 and is reputed to be the oldest house in the town.

St. Mary's
STAMFORD

CAGE
Alan Oliver

A village filled with surprises can be found tucked away on a country road between Stamford and Bourne. An essential stop for the visitor, Greatford is a very pretty spot with the River Glen running close by and contains a great deal to satisfy the curious, particularly the parish church, a distinctive building of the Early English and Decorated periods with a broach spire and dedicated to St. Thomas à Becket (1118-1170). His martyrdom in Canterbury Cathedral where he was murdered on the supposed orders of Henry II is remembered in a painting from 1959 by a former rector, the Rev R. Burman, which hangs inside.

There is also a ship's bell in the nave, presented in 1969 for safe keeping to mark the links between the village and *HMS Greatford* shortly before the warship was broken up.

A worshipper here in past times was Dr. Francis Willis, one of the most celebrated doctors from the 18th century who successfully treated King George III during one of his periods of madness in 1788 and was rewarded with an annual gratuity of £1,000 for 21 years. He ran a private asylum in the village, firstly at Greatford Hall which stands close to the church and later at Shillingthorpe Hall, built nearby for his son John around 1796.

Dr. Willis, who lived to be 90, was one of the most celebrateddoctors of his time, specialising in the treatment of *'afflicted persons of distinction and respectability'*. His patient list contained many titled people including a marquis and several honourables as well as a sprinkling of clergymen and doctors, who spent long periods undergoing treatment.

Greatford Hall closed as an asylum in 1838 and was burned down in 1922 but was sympathetically rebuilt and remains a private house while Shillingthorpe Hall closed in 1863 and, after various uses in the ensuing years, was demolished in 1949. The life of Dr. Willis is remembered after he was laid to rest here in 1807 with an impressive memorial plaque and bust in the transept by the finest of British sculptors, Joseph Nollekens (1737-1823).

St. Thomas à Becket Church

GREATFORD

Alan Oliver

The village of Corby Glen has had several schools in the past, the most illustrious being Read's Grammar School, a picturesque stone building founded in 1669 under the will of Charles Read (1604-1669), a wealthy Nottinghamshire shipper and merchant who bequeathed a yearly rent of £48 15s. 5½d. to pay for the instruction of village children in reading, writing, arithmetic and Latin.

In 1880, Queen Victoria approved a scheme for Read's Grammar School which provided for boarders and fixed the headmaster's yearly salary at £25 plus a fee for each boy attending the school. Boys were to be of *'good character and sufficient health'* and they were taught the

> *'principals of the Christian faith, reading, writing, arithmetic, geography, history, English grammar, composition and literature, mathematics, Latin, at least one foreign European language, natural science, drawing, drill and vocal music'.*

For 240 years, this school educated the more prosperous sons of the countryside until it closed in 1909, being unable to compete with larger schools made accessible by modern transport. In 1963 it was replaced by the new Charles Read Secondary School, but the old building is still in a fine state of repair having been restored and rededicated and it now houses the Willoughby Memorial Library and Art Gallery. The project that was opened on Friday 29th October 1965 in memory of Timothy, Lord Willoughby de Eresby (born 1936), son and heir apparent of the third Earl and Countess of Ancaster, of Grimsthorpe Castle, who went missing during a storm while boating in the Mediterranean between Cap Ferrat and Corsica on 20th August 1963 and was never seen again. As a result of the earl's intervention, the building was leased to the Willoughby Memorial Trust for 99 years and dedicated as a memorial to his son for all to use.

This is now an unusual sight in such a small village, listed Grade II as being a building of historic and architectural interest as well as being a popular public amenity containing a well stocked library and reading room with space available for local artists to display their work with six exhibitions a year between Easter and late autumn.

The Willoughby Memorial Library

CORBY GLEN

Alan Oliver.

Memories of the Mallard

LITTLE BYTHAM

The street scene at Little Bytham may appear unimposing but is a reminder to every railway buff of a world record set up during the last century by a steam locomotive travelling at more than two miles a minute which has remained unbroken ever since. The viaduct over the main street carries the east coast line between Grantham in Lincolnshire and Peterborough and it was on this stretch of track that the record was broken. On Sunday 3rd July 1938, the London and North Eastern Railway 4-6-2 engine No 4468 Mallard, a streamlined Gresley A4 Pacific, hauling seven coaches weighing 240 tons, achieved the highest speed ever ratified for a steam locomotive of 126 mph over a distance of 440 yards.

On the footplate were two Doncaster men, Driver Duddington at the controls and Fireman Thomas Bray feeding the boiler with coal. By the time the train swept through Little Bytham, the 6 ft 8 in driving wheels were doing more than 500 revolutions a minute – but it was not without cost for the engine was damaged by the severe exertions to which it had been subjected. It was forced to pull into the railway engineering workshops at Peterborough for repairs but nevertheless, the record was in the bag, exceeding the speed of 114 mph set up by the Coronation Scot the previous year, and remains so until this day.

The station at Little Bytham closed in 1969 but the village remains a popular haunt for lovers of railways and even the local public house that was once known as the Green Man, changed its name in 1975 to The Mallard. Although it closed in 2002 and is now a private residence, it has been called Mallard House as a reminder of the famous event. The stone building stands in the shadow of the grand Victorian viaduct that is still in use and, though it is inter-city express trains rather than steam engines which now flash past at regular intervals, this spot remains hallowed ground for railway enthusiasts of all ages who come here to photograph the scene or just to watch the trains go by.

Alan Oliver

The Village Stocks

WITHAM-ON-THE-HILL

The more callous forms of public punishment for wrongdoers have long been abandoned and the stocks are among them. Those that survive are a reminder of the retribution that awaited offenders for even the smallest transgression.

Witham-on-the-Hill is mentioned in the *Domesday Book,* the great land survey ordered by William the Conqueror in 1086 to assess land tax and other dues in his domain. It is, as the name suggests, on a hill with a steep incline leading to the village green and by the side of this large expanse of grass are the mediaeval stocks, preserved as a relic of the village's ancient past.

The stocks were a device for the punishment of certain criminals, often for trivial infringements of the law, and were usually the fate of vagabonds and other petty offenders. A tiled canopy protects the wooden baulks that were padlocked together to imprison the feet of miscreants for a set period and this suggests that justice at Witham was tempered with mercy for those incarcerated were protected from the elements. Once locked in for a set period, usually a few days, the unfortunate felons were liable to further indignities by being spat upon and pelted with rotten fruit and vegetables, sticks and stones, and therefore unlikely to escape unscathed after an ordeal they would remember for a very long time.

They were last used in England in the middle of the 19th century but here at Witham they are preserved as a reminder of the way it was and, of course, as a tourist attraction for the village's many visitors. These include the parents of pupils at the 18th century Witham Hall nearby. Hidden by high stone walls and hedges, it was once a grand house owned by a local landowner but is now an exclusive preparatory school for boys and girls.

The blue plaques on the wall alongside the stocks commemorate awards to the parish council in the Best Kept Village Competition which is held in the countryside every year to stimulate pride in the community and this is a very pretty village indeed.

Alan Oliver.

Alan Oliver

Bourne

Leaving Stamford and driving north-east on the A6121, the route takes us through gently sloping countryside of fields filled with growing crops, corn and flax, barley and oil seed, for we are now in the heart of the agricultural area for which this county is famous. Once through Toft village with its notoriously steep hill on a double bend, the land falls away to reveal the rooftops of Bourne and the fen beyond. The vantage point is Stamford Hill, scene of many bonfire celebrations in past times to mark victories in war and the accession of monarchs, and here the road joins the A151 for the last mile into town which is smaller than Stamford with a population of 15,000 and a more modest architectural heritage.

Bourne has always been associated with water, the very name indicating that this is a place near to the source of a spring or stream, first recorded in a document of about 960 as *Brunne*. Over the years this became Bourn and then in 1893 it was changed to Bourne to avoid confusion with other places of similar name, particularly Bourn in Cambridgeshire that had already caused difficulties with the postal and railway services.

The tower of the Abbey Church dominates South Street, founded by the Lord of the Manor, Baldwin Fitzgilbert, in the 12th century, probably around 1138, originally as a monastic house for an Augustinian order of canons. The present church, dedicated to St. Peter and St. Paul, has been extensively altered over the years and is the town's only Grade I listed building. There is evidence that it was to be built to cathedral-like proportions but the scheme was thwarted by the Black Death which claimed the lives of many working masons and did not therefore come to fruition and a second tower envisaged in the original plans was never built. The nave as far as the clerestory is a beautiful example of Norman work and the lower part of the tower also shows traces of this period while examples of other styles can be found throughout.

The coming of the railway during the 19th century played a major role in the expansion of the town, the system linking Bourne with the main east coast line at Essendine in 1860. By 1894, Bourne had become a railway centre of some importance and was connected to the Midlands and East Anglia, thus enabling the movement of passengers and freight throughout the country and giving many people their first glimpse of the seaside through day excursions to Hunstanton and Skegness. But the steam age boom was not to last and despite protests from local people, the final passenger train left in February 1959 and freight services were withdrawn in 1965.

There is evidence of a castle in Bourne and tradition decrees that the hills and hollows that can be seen in the Wellhead Gardens are the site of this building which was the birthplace of Hereward the Wake, son of the Earl Leofric of Mercia and his wife Lady Godiva. He owned the manor of Bourne and lead the Saxon uprising against the invaders after the Norman Conquest of 1066, although his reputation rests mainly with the many fictional tales of his exploits from Victorian writers. After being outlawed for the rough treatment of certain monks at Peterborough, young Hereward had many incredible adventures in Britain and the Low Countries before returning home to challenge the Normans and clearing them from Bourne. There are accounts of an untimely death at the hands of the enemy in the woods near Bourne but there is no conclusive evidence about his activities after being routed by the Normans in 1071 and his fate is unknown. Ancient tradition suggests that he was buried in the chancel at Bourne Abbey but there is no evidence of such a tomb existing.

Few buildings predate the 17th century because of two serious fires which devastated the town. On 23rd August 1605, a blaze broke out in Manor Street and raged for three days and not a house was left standing, a disaster so serious that King James I set up a national appeal to help relieve the distress. Then on 25th March 1637 another outbreak destroyed the Eastgate area of the town, home to a thriving pottery industry which never fully recovered. Despite this setback, Bourne still has a lot of old and interesting architecture and there are currently a total of 71 listed properties, while the main amenity within the Conservation Area is the Wellhead Gardens, established on 21 acres of meadow under the terms of a bequest from a local farmer together with the Garden of Remembrance and the War Memorial which were opened in 1956.

The Wellhead Gardens are just a short step from the town centre but a place of peace and tranquillity favoured by walkers and office workers enjoying a sandwich break and even the occasional lunchtime tryst. There is a particular delight in springtime when the white and pink flowering cherry trees that line the main path burst into blossom to create a colourful avenue for visitors and many are so enchanted by the sight that they retrace their steps to take another look.

A grammar school has existed in Bourne since the Middle Ages and in the early 17th century William Trollope, a local landowner, left a bequest which provided for an endowment of £30 a year to maintain *'an honest, learned, and godly schoolmaster'* in a free grammar school incorporated by royal charter. The present building in the churchyard dates from 1678, probably on the site of a previous one, and continued in use until 1904 when it closed. Since used for short spells as a Sunday School, ambulance station and a meeting place for boy scouts and girl guides, it now stands empty and up for sale and, although Grade II listed, it has restricted access and the future for its survival is distinctly bleak. The present Bourne Grammar School was founded in 1920 and now occupies extensive premises in South Road, a flagship educational establishment where places are highly sought after.

The old Grammar School, Bourne

Wake House, built in North Street in 1810, is the only building in Bourne to carry a coveted blue plaque, installed in December 2002 at the instigation of English Heritage to remember Charles Worth (1825-1895), the famous Paris designer and father of haute couture who was born here. Other famous people who have connections with this town include Raymond Mays (1899-1980), international racing driver and designer who founded English Racing Automobiles (ERA) followed by British Racing Motors (BRM) which in 1962 became the first all British car to win the world championship with Graham Hill at the wheel. A stone memorial erected in 2003 can be found in South Street commemorating this remarkable period that brought fame to the town and also provided employment opportunities because at one time the company's workshops had a staff of 100.

The history of the town's four hospitals has been one of useful service but all are now closed. The earliest was a fever hospital established in two empty cottages in Manor Lane to accommodate cases during a smallpox outbreak in 1885 and continued in use until 1913 when Bourne Urban District Council began work on a new hospital in South Road which was opened in the summer of 1915. By 1965, it was being run as a medical and surgical unit with 53 beds and a full range of services but was shut despite a vigorous protest campaign by local people who raised a petition containing 8,000 names. The battle was eventually lost in 1998 and the premises were left standing empty for the next five years before being demolished and the land swallowed up by new housing. St. Peter's Hospital for the mentally handicapped was established in 1930 in the former workhouse premises in St. Peter's Road but patients were moved out under the government's policy of care in the community and the entire complex sold for commercial development in 1997 and demolished four years later.

The Butterfield Hospital was opened in 1910 in a converted private house in North Road known as Brooklands which was bequeathed to the community by Mr Joseph Butterfield who once lived there. It soon became a valued medical amenity for the town and district, enlarged in 1920 as a memorial to those who died in the Great War of 1914-18 and continuing in use until 1982 when it was shut down despite public protest. Lincolnshire County Council was eventually persuaded to buy the building in 1985 when it began its present role as the Butterfield Day Care Centre for the elderly.

There has been a weekly market in Bourne for more than 700 years under a Royal Charter granted to the Lord of the Manor of Bourne, Baldwin Wake, by King Edward I in 1279, giving permission for it to be held on a Saturday and this tradition has continued to the present day although there is now another on a Thursday. Traders originally erected their stalls on the streets but moved to a new paved area behind the Town Hall in 1991 because of the danger to shoppers from increasing traffic flows. A weekly cattle market was also held in Bourne for more than a century but closed in 1981 because of increasingly restrictive EEC regulations and the site was replaced by the Burghley Arcade development which opened between 1988-90.

Agriculture dominates the local economy of the town which is surrounded by thousands of productive acres devoted to a variety of crops while processing factories nearby supply our major supermarket chains. Corn is the predominant crop, as it has been in years past, and the cause of civil unrest in the 18th century. The corn riot occurred in 1740 when a gang of angry townspeople tried to prevent a consignment of grain from being sent by barge to Spalding along the Bourne Eau. This was a year of rising prices and a scarcity of food and they resented corn grown locally going to feed people in other parts of the country when they themselves were hungry. John Halford of Bourne wrote to local landowner Sir John Heathcote at his residence in Epping Forest:

> *'We have had a Disturbance by the Mobb at Bourne. They cutt some sacks of wheat in the boat and obstructed its passage to Spalding for a time but was quel'd seasonably by Officers of the Town and five women committed to the House of Correction* [at Folkingham].'

Brick-making was also a major industry during the late 19th century to meet the demand created by a boom in house building from yards on the north and west side of Bourne but the industry did not survive into the 20th century. The town was also a major producer of water cress sending regular supplies by rail to markets in London and Leicester but the cress beds were eventually closed in 1974. Today, other industries have come to prominence with printing among the most important, Warners Midlands plc having grown from a small newsagents business to a major producer of magazines employing some 400 people.

The Abbey Church was founded in 1138 as a monastic house and was also home to two learned canons or monks who lived the cloistered life and are credited with helping mould the English language we speak today. Orm the Preacher (flourished 1180) wrote a homily collection known as *The Ormulum* providing a glimpse of the English vernacular of the time and his manuscript is now in the Bodleian Library at Oxford University.

Robert Manning (1264-1340), also known as Robert de Brunne, is credited with putting the speech of the ordinary people of his time into the recognisable form that we know today. He completed his life's work while a canon at Bourne Abbey and in the process popularised religious and historical material in a Middle English dialect that was easily understood by the people of his time. His most familiar work was *Handlyng Synne,* a book of great value because it gives glimpses into the ways and thoughts of our countrymen 700 years ago.

The monastic life, however, was not always as austere as is generally believed and the Vicar-General, John Rayne, found a most unsatisfactory state of affairs when he visited Bourne in 1525, raising a formidable list of complaints against the Abbot, John Small, claiming that he had lost his influence and discipline had gone. It was alleged that he had not been rendering the necessary accounts with the result that rents suffered and that the monks, instead of retiring early as was the custom of the abbey, often came downstairs again and sat drinking until the early hours, so making them late for matins next day.

Nor did they keep the silence as they should have done and lay people were freely allowed into the monastic buildings, even in the dormitory where tailors and cobblers gathered to mend and repair their clothes and shoes. Several were disobedient, one spoke insulting words to the abbot and another insisted on having a fire in his room where he could lie in comfort rather than go to services while others neither sang, nor read but spent their time drinking, making merry and gossiping early and late.

The Abbey Church

BOURNE

Alan Oliver

The longest serving tenant of the 17th century Red Hall was Catherine Digby who went there as a young bride in 1796 and remained in occupation until her death in 1836. Her husband, James Digby, a wealthy land-owner, was almost forty years her senior and when he died in 1811, she took over the house and his estates.

By this time she had become a rich lady, playing an influential part in the affairs of the town, a thoughtful benefactress who liked to be known as Lady of the Manor while enjoying her life at the Red Hall and tending the beautiful garden she created there.

She died childless on 29th February 1836, aged 63, and was given a grand funeral to which the entire town turned out. She was the last private resident to own and live in the Red Hall which was rented out to various tenants and even had a spell as a private school before being sold to the Bourne and Essendine Railway Company for use as a booking office at the new railway station and it remained as such until the line closed in 1959. The building stood empty for several years until acquired by the present owners, Bourne United Charities, in 1962 and is now used as their offices although some of the main rooms are rented out for private functions.

Catherine was buried in the chancel of the Abbey Church and in the years since her death, there have been stories that the Red Hall is haunted by a grey lady who flits through the rooms on moonlit nights – a tale no doubt perpetuated, as with other country houses in England, because of the combination of light and shade that we get on moonlit nights and the tendency of those who tell of them to invariably elaborate. No one seems to have suggested who this phantom might be but as no other woman had such a long connection with the house, perhaps Catherine, who was so reluctant to leave, would be first choice as the ghost of the Red Hall.

The Red Hall

BOURNE

Alan Oliver

There were six water mills in Bourne when the *Domesday Book* was compiled in 1086 but only one, Baldock's Mill, remains. It stands on the banks of the Bourne Eau, the present building dating from 1800. Farmers brought their corn here to be ground using two sets of stones operating on the first floor and fed by hoppers from above, the grain being lifted by a chain hoist, all driven by a water wheel whose power was increased in later years by making alterations to the course of the river outside.

The name of the mill changed with the passing of time, usually adopted from the last miller who worked there, in this case Frederick Baldock whose family had a sixty-year association. It was during his tenure in 1924 that the water wheel collapsed and the owner, the Marquess of Exeter, who called in experts to inspect the damage, decided not to repair it because of the high costs involved. The machinery was subsequently removed although the importance of the building was recognised in 1977 when it was listed Grade II as being of historic and architectural importance. Ownership passed to Bourne United Charities and after various uses in the intervening years, Bourne Civic Society was granted the lease for a peppercorn rent in 1981 and members set about a programme of restoration.

Today it has a new lease of life as the town's Heritage Centre housing several exhibitions relating to its past, notably the lives of Bourne's two famous sons, fashion designer Charles Worth and international racing driver Raymond Mays. Other features include extensive displays on the importance of the aerated water industry and the steam railway age together with artefacts preserved from various sources and reflecting the local history from previous centuries.

The water wheel has also been restored to its original use and in 2007 began turning again to produce green electricity to light the mill and help reduce maintenance costs, a project undertaken entirely by volunteers and the success of the Heritage Centre is reflected in the many awards it has received.

Baldock's Mill

BOURNE

Alan Oliver

The Angel Hotel in the town centre dates from the 18th century and was originally known as the Nag's Head but the name was changed around 1800. It was an important posting house when Bourne was on the main route between London and the north and a daily stage coach service connecting with Lincoln and York passed through, often making an overnight stop and usually picking up travellers. More than one baby was born there after lady passengers went into labour during the journey.

The livery stables at the rear of the building were eventually incorporated into the main hotel and by 1900 it boasted fifteen bedrooms and a banqueting room that could accommodate 150 people. During the 19th century, beer sold in the hotel bars was produced by a small brewery at the rear of the premises and the old ostler's bell used by arriving stage coaches to summon help can still be seen in the courtyard while outside on the main road, the town pump was strategically placed to provide for the needs of the horses.

Apart from its function as a hotel, the Angel was also registered as an Excise Office from 1808 onwards where makers of a wide range of goods were required to pay their necessary duties.

In 1862, the Assembly Rooms were erected in the courtyard at the rear of the hotel in matching red brick and blue slate by the landlord, Henry Bott (1810-1888), and the date with his initials appear on a stone plaque at the front. The new facility was used for a wide range of social events, dances and parties, and as the meeting hall for many local organisations, including the Hereward Lodge of Freemasons (No. 1232) which was formed there in 1868.

The rooms have been known in recent years and used for public functions and wedding receptions while the disused outbuildings and stables at the rear of the hotel were converted into a new shopping centre called the Angel Walk in 1985.

The Angel Hotel

BOURNE

ANGEL
HOTEL
Alan Oliver

The lake on the edge of the Wellhead Gardens is known as St. Peter's Pool, fed by seven underground springs that never dry up. It is this constant water source that became the centre of the ancient community that grew into the town of Bourne and was also reputed to have curative properties. A century ago one of the most important of these chalybeate springs was at nearby Braceborough Spa where it gushed from the limestone at the rate of a million and a half gallons daily. There was another source five miles to the west at Holywell and another at Stoke Rochford, places that were said to *'abound in springs of pure water rising out of the rock and running into the River Witham'.*

St. Peter's Pool, also known as the Wellhead, is one of the most ancient sites of artesian water supplies in the country, figuring prominently in the history of the town and at times remarkable traditions have gathered around it. One of these still current in the mid-19th century suggested that the Bourne Eau, the river which flows from the pool, actually came underground from Stoke Rochford, sixteen miles away, and that a white duck which was immersed at Stoke was later seen to rise at the Wellhead.

The town has provided an abundant supply of pure water since the earliest times and during the 19th century generated a new business when Robert Mason Mills (1819-1904), a local chemist, realised the potential and began bottling it in 1864. His aerated water products were soon acclaimed world wide and even awarded a Royal Warrant for supplying Queen Victoria's son, the Duke of Connaught, while large quantities were sent out to British soldiers during the Egyptian campaign in 1882. The company continued until well into the next century and spawned several others while the natural springs underneath the town were soon being exploited by 140 artesian boreholes and although supplies remain plentiful today, they are now extracted and controlled by Anglian Water and piped to a much larger catchment area.

St. Peter's Pool

BOURNE

One of the most attractive areas of natural beauty in the area comprises some 400 acres of ancient woodland known as Bourne Wood which is now managed for conservation as well as recreation and timber production. The Forestry Commission bought the larger part of the wood from the Earl of Exeter, the Lord of the Manor, in 1926 and the timber produced an income of 20 shillings per acre per annum, most of it being used for fencing enclosures.

In the preceding years, the woods had been heavily felled, most probably to provide props for the trenches during the First World War, and there was an urgent need for extensive replanting. When the commission took over, part of their policy was to plant softwoods because the return on them was much quicker but this system has since been reviewed and the loss of broad-leaved trees is being remedied under a new programme of bringing back the old forest.

Bourne Wood has become a major tourist attraction in recent years with over 100,000 visitors a year. Many plants have survived and so make the area valuable in terms of wildlife conservation. The wild flowers that can be seen here in season include bluebells, primroses, wood anemone and nettle-leaved bell flower while fallow deer are abundant and you may catch a glimpse of their smaller, shy cousin, the muntjac or barking deer. Other animals that can be seen in these glades are foxes, grey squirrels, owls, snakes, badgers and dormice and a wide variety of birds. Nightingales can be heard on summer nights and dragonflies fly over the ponds at twilight. Seven species of bat have also been identified including the rare Leisler's bat which was first discovered in nesting boxes in 1991 and is now being closely monitored by the Forestry Commission in conjunction with English Nature.

The woodland has many paths and trails, some leading to the more remote parts of the forest, including two lakes at the further end where fallow deer can be seen watering in the early morning and at dusk, while sculpture trails add a cultural interest in various places.

Bourne Wood

BOURNE

Alan Oliver

There is a long history of charity to the poor in Bourne through the benevolence of wealthy people and the almshouses in South Street remind us of this philanthropy.

A stone tablet on the front of the Tudor Cottages in South Street suggests that these almshouses were built in 1636 but this is misleading as they most likely date from the late 18th or early 19th century. The date 1636 refers to the first buildings on this site which were the Trollope Bedehouses. The present cottages were built on the original foundations and much of the material from the previous properties was probably used in the reconstruction.

A stone tablet on the front of the Tudor Cottages in South Street suggests that these almshouses were built in 1636 but this is misleading as they most likely date from the late 18th or early 19th century. 1636 refers to the first buildings on this site which were the Trollope Bedehouses. The present cottages were built on the original foundations and much of the material from the previous properties was probably used in the reconstruction.

The benefactor for this charitable undertaking was William Trollope, a landowner, and member of a prominent wealthy family which had been associated with the Bourne area since 1543. He founded a hospital and provided a yearly sum of £33 for the maintenance of *'six poor aged men'* from the parish who were accommodated in the almshouses. Trollope was also instrumental in providing sufficient funds to help put education on a firm footing and his generosity was typical of several rich landowners of the period who contributed greatly to the welfare of the people and the development of the town.

Two major charitable organisations also reflect the generosity of past inhabitants. Bourne United Charities administers several bequests from past years and has been responsible for twelve almshouses and a warden's bungalow in West Street since they opened in 1932 to provide homes for elderly inhabitants while the Len Pick Trust distributes regular grants from the £4 million fortune left more recently by a local landowner and businessman.

The South Street Almshouses

BOURNE

Alan Oliver

The earliest reference to a town hall can be found in a description of Bourne by the 16th century historian William Camden in 1586 although the present building dates from 1821, designed by the architect Bryan Browning (1773-1856) who decided on an exterior staircase of Portland stone and recessed twin flights of steps within the front of the building that was to be constructed with Doric columns after the fashion of the Roman baths. The work was financed by public subscription and a list of 122 of the district's great and good who made contributions totalling almost £1,400 can be found inscribed on a large board inside and includes landowners, clergymen, shopkeepers, tradesmen, law officers and even the chief constable.

Since then, the building has been in constant use, for meetings of the manorial courts which controlled land and property and heard grievances, as a magistrates court and Quarter Sessions which dispensed justice and, in more recent years, as offices for the district and town councils.

The town's fire station was once situated underneath one of the arches with a bell and rope pull outside to raise the alarm while the horses to tow the fire appliance were stabled at the Bull Hotel next door (now the Burghley Arms). The horses were shared with the local undertaker who used them to haul his hearse at funerals. During the 19th century, the Town Hall was frequently in demand for functions and many of the district's big social events were held there as well as grand dances that were enjoyable but frequently tiring occasions when the revelry continued throughout the night with coaches to take guests home not needed until the early hours.

There was originally a tower with a clock which, from 1899 was illuminated by a gas lamp, but one Saturday afternoon in late October 1933 the mechanism became overheated and set light to the wooden turret which was destroyed beyond repair despite valiant efforts by firemen to save it. It was never replaced and the clock was later reinstalled on the pediment below where it can be seen today.

The Town Hall

BOURNE

A plaque on the front of the Burghley Arms records that this was the birthplace on 13th September 1520 of the distinguished statesman William Cecil, Lord High Treasurer during the reign of Queen Elizabeth I who became the first Lord Burghley. He built Burghley House at Stamford for his home, thus cementing the link between there and his birthplace which he remembered by bestowing a new town hall on the town, replaced in 1821 by the present stone building which dominates of North Street in what is now the town centre.

In William Cecil's day, the Burghley Arms, with its distinctive dormer windows overlooking the market place, was a private house but in 1717 was converted for use as a coaching inn known as the Bull and Swan, shortened to the Bull in the 19th century and in 1955 changed to its present name in honour of Lord Burghley. The traditional arch through which the stage coaches passed to reach the stables at the rear has been filled in to make way for an entrance to the lounge bar while a particular feature that has been retained to lend a horizontal emphasis to the facade is the fine pair of stone mullioned windows on the ground floor, each with six leaded lights and the central or 'king' mullions thickened to take the weight.

In more recent times, the Burghley Arms was home to a prominent writer from the First World War who also had close connections with the town. He was the Australian born Frederick Manning (1882-1935), author of *Her Privates We,* a highly acclaimed novel about life in the trenches during the Battle of the Somme which is still in print today. The name chosen for his hero was Private Bourne after the town where he had spent such happy times and where, despite failing health and oxygen cylinders within easy reach, he had completed much of the original manuscript in his diminutive handwriting while staying as a paying guest at the Bull and later as a lodger with a family in Burghley Street.

The Burghley Arms

BOURNE

THE BURGHLEY ARMS
Alan Oliver

Felons brought before the magistrates at Stamford or Bourne in past times who were given a custodial sentence, invariably ended up at the House of Correction at Folkingham, a forbidding place where both men and women were sent as a punishment for wrongdoing. The building that survives replaces an earlier one which became unfit for its original purpose and after conditions had been condemned by social reformers during the late 18th century, a local architect, Bryan Browning, the man responsible for the Town Hall at Bourne, was retained to design new premises.

The first phase was completed in 1808 with several later additions to provide accommodation for 70 prisoners and prison officers. Inside there was a chapel and the entrance to the cells was through the dining room while the entire prison was surrounded by a high wall. The imposing gatehouse was intended to be a powerful warning for those who entered, a symbolic attempt to avert or turn away evil, and indeed those who arrived did so with some trepidation. Prisoners were taken there from the courts with iron manacles for the unruly and troublesome while even more sinister conditions were to be found inside for those who defied the strict regime with several punishment devices including a treadmill, a whipping post and stocks capable of holding three miscreants at a time.

The prison closed in 1878 when the remaining prisoners were transferred elsewhere and the premises were used for a time as temporary accommodation for homeless villagers.

The only part of the original building now remaining is the gatehouse and governor's quarters, preserved at the end of an impressive driveway with wrought iron entrance gates. It also has a very different role today being owned by the Landmark Trust, an organisation that seeks out unusual and empty properties throughout Britain and turns them into holiday accommodation with all mod cons. Thus the House of Correction has became a favourite stopping place with visitors from America and Japan while the stocks and whipping post have been preserved in the west end of the nave of the village church as a reminder of its gruesome history.

The House of Correction

FOLKINGHAM

HOUSE OF CORRECTION A.D
Alan Oliver

The name of Sempringham was once known throughout the land but today it is a difficult place to find, well off the beaten track at the end of an isolated farm road but once there, the rewards are great because St. Andrew's Church remains a reminder of a celebrated event in our history.

This is the site of the famous St. Mary's Priory founded by the crippled priest St. Gilbert in about 1139 as a home for his white-robed Gilbertian order, the only purely English monastic order and the only one which catered for men and women alike. It was situated to the south of the present church but was destroyed in 1558 and all that remains today are signs of earthworks, although excavations have revealed the foundations together with fish ponds and an old water source, now preserved as the Holy Well. Remains of stained glass, pottery, coins and carved masonry have also been found and stones from the original buildings are thought to have been used in the construction of some houses in the locality.

A few yards to the south of the church stands a stone and slate memorial which honours the mediaeval Princess Gwenllian (1283-1337), daughter of Llewellyn, the last true born Prince of Wales and the only grand-daughter of Simon de Montfort.

Gwenllian was held captive here for more than half a century, being imprisoned when she was only 17 months old by Edward I fearing that she might threaten his suzerainty over Wales. He wrote to the Prior and Prioress of the abbey which then stood on the site asking them to admit her to the order and the habit. Then in 1327, when Edward III stayed at Sempringham, he granted Gwenllian a yearly pension of £20 for life. She died ten years later on 7th June 1337 after 54 years of virtual imprisonment by the order. The memorial was erected in 1993 by the Princess Gwenllian Society and later blessed by the Bishop of Bangor. Although vandalised in 2000, it has been replaced and coach loads of Welsh pilgrims continue to visit the site to pay their respects.

St. Andrew's Church

SEMPRINGHAM

Alan Oliver

The Baptist Chapel

Haconby

The most insignificant buildings in some of our villages are often worth a second look and so it is with the Baptist Chapel at Haconby, built in 1867 and now the smallest galleried chapel of worship in England, being only 24 ft long and a mere 13 ft 6 in wide. It was originally intended to seat 100 people on the ground floor but it was finished 18 inches narrower in width than was planned and was clearly too small.

The builder admitted that he was at fault and when told that he must remedy the error, made up for the lost seating room by adding two galleries facing each other. They were so close together that worshippers could actually shake hands with each other if they so wished, as many do today. This tiny chapel of red brick and blue slate was built in the main street on a piece of land owned by Mr W Brown Senior, the site being in the far corner of the grounds of the house where he lived and a brown plaque with white lettering over the door records his philanthropy.

It was originally used by the United Baptists and the Primitive Methodists, both non-conformist religious groups with a strong working class bias, but after thirty years, around 1899, the Baptists took it over completely. A peppercorn rent of £1 a year was paid to Mr Brown and later to his son, but when he died on 21st July 1932, his estate, including the chapel, was put up for sale.

The solicitors handling his affairs did not agree with the view that the chapel had been intended as a gift to the village and the auction sale of the property, held at the Angel Hotel in Bourne, was held up for fifteen minutes by discussion and argument over the issue. In the end, the chapel was withdrawn from sale on the condition that £50 was paid to secure the building for permanent ownership. The people of Haconby managed to raise the money and the chapel has been in public use ever since.

Alan Oliver.

Eight hundred years of history are to be found just a short distance from Bourne at Grimsthorpe Castle, home of the de Eresby family since 1516 when it was granted by Henry VIII to the 11th Baron Willoughby de Eresby on the occasion of his marriage to Maria de Salinas, lady in waiting to the Queen, Katherine of Aragon. The early history of the house is connected with the Cistercian Abbey of Vaudy, founded in 1147, which once stood to the south of the lake and the house, itself built in the late 13th century by Gilbert de Gant, while monks from the monastery are believed to be buried in the churchyard at nearby Creeton.

The oldest part of the building is the south east corner of the castle called King John's Tower which dates back to 1199-1216 while the parkland was landscaped by Capability Brown in 1771. The formal flower and topiary garden leads imperceptibly into a woodland area and provides a fine setting for the ornamental vegetable garden and orchard, created in the 1960s by the Countess of Ancaster and John Fowler. The main state rooms and the chapel at Grimsthorpe are all furnished with many objects of rare, artistic and historical interest, including coronation robes, chairs and canopies of George I–IV and Queen Victoria, and are open to view. Paintings by Van Dyck, Holbein and Reynolds are among the most notable pictures together with the rare tapestries in the state dining room.

Grimsthorpe has been the location for several major television productions and is a popular place with visitors.

The house is surrounded by extensive parkland, once the southern edge of a great forest, together with rolling pastures, landscaped lakes and historic woodland. Many of the great oaks growing here were felled during Tudor times for building ships in the Queen's navy while some of those which can be seen today were planted after the restoration of the Stuart monarchy, the avenues creating a haven for wildlife. There was horse racing here in the 18th century and a nine-hole golf course in the 1920s while troops were camped here prior to the Arnhem airborne invasion during the Second World War.

Grimsthorpe Castle

EDENHAM

Alan Oliver

The Deepings

Farming links Bourne to the Deepings, the collective name given to those small communities that lie to the south, Market Deeping, Deeping St. James and the outlying Deeping Gate, all bordering the banks of the River Welland as it meanders between Lincolnshire and Cambridgeshire, with West Deeping detached but not entirely isolated from the rest.

Crop production hereabouts has always been dependent on the drainage of the fens, a project which began with the Romans to prevent flooding and enable the land to remain productive in all weather, although the major activity was during the 17th and 18th centuries led by Dutch engineers. It was financed by speculators (or adventurers as they were known), wealthy landowners anxious to use their land holdings to the full. Today the countryside is still crisscrossed with dykes and drainage ditches although the many windmills which studded the skyline in past times have been replaced by remote controlled pumping stations that regulate the levels in times of heavy rain while controversial wind turbines are now appearing on the skyline to generate electricity.

The route to the Deepings lies south east along the main A15 trunk road from Bourne which runs directly into Market Deeping. A stone bridge marks the route out of town and on to Peterborough for Market Deeping stands on the very edge of the county border with Cambridgeshire. The bridge which carries the A15 over the River Welland was opened in July 1842 and the firm that built it was made bankrupt by the contract. There had been a wooden bridge at this point since the 16th century and is mentioned in the survey of 1563 as either the Wheat Bridge or the Blind Bridge and there is a further reference in parish documents relating to repair work which was carried out in the years 1585-87.

There was a distillery here, established by local doctors William Holland and William Page in the early years of the 19th century to produce essential oils from herbs and other plants for the manufacture of medicines, ointments, lotions and liniments to treat the variety of ailments and physical conditions that afflicted Victorian society. The venture began in a small way with one copper urn out in the open air and later from a small shed with a thatched roof before a permanent distillery was built in 1836. Soon, several hundred acres were being used for the cultivation of a variety of herbs such as hemlock and rosemary, belladonna, henbane, peppermint and poppy while the fields of lavender when in bloom were reckoned to be particularly beautiful. The essential oils they produced were sold throughout England and abroad, winning medals at many international exhibitions in London, Paris and Berlin, while the products were endorsed by the leading apothecaries of the day on account of their excellent quality. The cultivation of herbs continued as a flourishing industry and even spawned a similar business in the United States but production ceased in the early years of the 20th century and the distillery was finally demolished in 2006. The site was developed for new housing although the venture is remembered in various streets which are named after herbs while one has been called Still Close.

Attractive stone bridges in the Deepings

There was also a gasworks here during the 19th century. Built by solicitor Francis Brown in 1855 to provide the district with heating and lighting, the installation consisted of two gasometers, a retort house and a tall chimney to disperse the smoke. The business became a limited company known as the Market Deeping Coal and Gas Light Company in 1868 when 300 tons of coal a year were brought in by rail and consumed to keep pace with production. However the demand for gas declined during the 20th century and soon alternative supplies were being piped in from Stamford and the gasworks was finally demolished in the years following the Second World War and although a remaining building was used for a short time as the village fire station, that too was eventually pulled down to make way for a block of apartments.

The crossroads in the town centre is completed by the A16 between Stamford and Spalding but is little more than a straggle of shops and business premises as the road runs eastwards with a side turn branching off into Deeping St. James and out into the fen beyond.

One of the most interesting buildings in Bridge Street is the old Baptist chapel, now a private house. In 1838, the vicar, the Rev Frederick Tryon, decided rather late in the day that he could not accept the Church of England's ancient teaching regarding infant baptism and took drastic action by ordering materials for the construction of a new chapel. As the building went up on a site overlooking the river, parishioners thought at first that a new vicarage was intended but eventually discovered that it was a Particular Baptist foundation which opened the following year. On 18th December 1840, the *Stamford Mercury* reported a mass baptism by total immersion of Baptist members in the river that excited tremendous interest in the neighbourhood. The report noted that the Reverend Tryon had seceded from the Church of England and had become a dissenter.

The Reverend Tryon left a remarkable legacy in many respects. Having not only started his own school, he also stuck to his little church, his active connection only ceasing on his death in 1903 when in his 90th year and long after that, his daughter could be seen going about her business around the Deepings on her tricycle. The chapel is now in private ownership and tastefully converted for residential use but a stone tablet over the main door bearing the opening date 1839 and the Latin motto *Cave Adullam* [Beware of Flattery] has been retained.

The Waterton Arms which can be found in Church Street and was formerly known as the Wheatsheaf, is a reminder of the village's connections with a distinguished family reckoned to be one of the oldest in Lincolnshire and the inn uses their coat of arms on its sign. Charles Waterton was a highly respected naturalist who travelled widely in South America during the early years of the 19th century and later established a collection of birds and animals at his home in Yorkshire. The family had originally lived in Lincolnshire and in 1877, his son Edmund Waterton, who was proud of his lineage and claimed to be a descendant of Sir Thomas More (1478-1535), the renaissance writer, statesman and Catholic martyr, returned to the county to buy the 18th century manor house at Deeping St. James and, believing that his ancestors had once owned the property, named it Waterton Hall and added two new wings. In 1880 he also built a small Roman Catholic chapel adjacent to the hall, dedicating it to Our Lady of Lincoln and St. Guthlac.

Edmund, who was twice married, soon established a reputation as the squire, a kindly gentleman and great sportsman who organised many events in the 26 acres of parkland surrounding his home as well as water sports on the river. He died tragically at the age of 48 while participating in one of the very events he had helped to arrange when in July 1887, during a sports meeting in the park to celebrate Queen Victoria's Golden Jubilee, he insisted on entering some of the athletic competitions. He was participating in one of the tug of war contests when the rope broke and he fell badly and was fatally injured. After his death, Waterton Hall was sold at auction and ownership passed to the Marquess of Exeter, becoming known once again as the manor house before being demolished in 1970.

Founded by the Benedictines and consecrated in 1139, the Priory Church is an impressive building of unexpected size with an early 18th century tower and a lead spire that can be seen ten miles away. The disparity of dates is due to a disaster that occurred in 1717 when the original church tower collapsed after foundations had rotted as a result of flooding in past times but was rebuilt with financial help from other parishes.

Many visitors to this area miss Deeping St. James because of its isolated location off the main A15 yet a diversion can be rewarding because this village has one of the most beautiful riverside walks in the county with the River Welland running alongside the main street and both banks accessible for much of its length with a pavement on one side and a footpath on the other which also connects with Deeping Gate, a small community of a few houses and bungalows on the road into Cambridgeshire.

Deeping Gate was also known as Deeping St. Mary because it was believed that a chapel once stood at the rear of Fairfax House, the grand stone residence at the foot of the bridge on the Cambridgeshire side and known in recent years as the doctor's house until the practice moved to the new medical centre in 1976. The original property was the home of Thomas, the third Lord Fairfax, leading general of the Parliamentary Army during the Civil War which led to the execution of Charles I and the accession of Cromwell as Lord Protector, but Fairfax wanted none of it and withdrew to private life, building his new home at Deeping Gate.

West Deeping is a little further south on the other side of the A16 and has barely a hundred houses but is a beautiful 'chocolate box cover' of a village with stone cottages, a water mill and church which dates back 750 years. There has been a settlement here since prehistoric times and the present village is one of the most secluded yet picturesque in the area. It is the smallest of the three Deepings on the southern edge of Lincolnshire, lying in a crook of the River Welland and set back from the high road linking its neighbours.

The best view of St. Andrew's, the parish church, is across the meadows from the one-arch bridge over the river while the mellow stone houses of the village line nearly half a mile of the old Roman road known as King Street which crosses the river here on its straight and narrow way northward to Bourne. The church is mainly 14th and 15th century and the present tower and spire were probably built around 1370 while the clerestory was added towards the close of the 15th century and the aisles rebuilt. The outstanding feature of the centre aisle is a magnificent large brass chandelier of twenty-four lights, almost identical to that in the Abbey Church at Bourne and most probably of Dutch origin.

One of the widest and prettiest thoroughfares in South Lincolnshire is Church Street, Market Deeping, with old stone buildings on either side and dominated by the embattled tower of St. Guthlac's Church. The architecture is mainly 15th century but much of it is earlier and a blocked arch in the north wall of the chancel is probably Saxon. The porch is 13th century and shelters a modern door, ornate with the original ironwork of slender leaf pattern. In two richly canopied niches by the altar are modern figures of St. Hugh of Lincoln and St. Guthlac, patron saint of this church, who came to nearby Crowland more than twelve centuries ago to establish Christianity in this wild place.

Ten medallions in two of the chancel windows tell the story of his life but this connection failed to prevent frequent friction between the Lords of Deeping and their tenants on the one hand and Crowland Abbey on the other, mainly over land rights in the surrounding fenland. In 1380, for instance, during a boundary dispute, the men of Deeping tore down the marker crosses, ripped up the abbot's fishing nets, held up the provision wagons, beat up his servants and threw his boatmen into the river. Like *'roaring whelps of lions'* they lay in wait to vent their malice on any monk from Crowland incautious enough to pass that way and it was only a rumoured threat that orders had been issued to the authorities to burn Deeping to the ground and slay the inhabitants that reduced them to acquiescence.

Next to the church is the old rectory dating from the 14th century when it was built by the monks although additions were made circa 1830 by Thomas Pilkington. Incumbents have reputedly been driven from the house twice, once by vagrants during the 16th century when the rector was forced to live in the church tower and again during the Civil War of 1642-49. In recent years it was known to successive clergymen and their wives as the coldest house in Lincolnshire although it has now been converted for use as two private homes with all modern conveniences.

MARKET DEEPING

Alan Oliver

The Market Place

MARKET DEEPING

As the name suggests, Market Deeping has always been essentially a market town, a charter being granted by the young Henry III in 1220 to William Briwer, an itinerant justice, who was related to the Wake family by marriage, to hold a market in the Manor of Deeping every week on a Thursday, but in 1300 Edward I granted Baron John Wake the charter and when he died, the rights passed to his widow, Joan Wake. However, the traditional market was moved off the streets to a nearby pedestrian precinct in the interests of road safety in the late 20th century while the fairs once held three times a year are no more.

The market place we see today is modern, being completed in April 2001 at a cost of £500,000 to make it more convenient for shoppers and vehicles while the entire area is decorated with hanging baskets to welcome visitors during the summer months. The street façades bear evidence of the town's 19th century prosperity with many fine stone built houses that were once the homes of wealthy merchants, now converted for use as shops, offices, banks and building societies.

Among them is the town hall, the first being recorded here as early as 1563 when it was also used as a court house but new premises were proposed in the early 19th century and the public was invited to help foot the bill. Thirty-nine subscriptions were received, including £20 each from the rector, the Rev William Hillyard, and Mr William Goodale, a local businessman, and the new building was erected in 1839 at a cost of £320. Felons were kept in the cells below until the police station across the road was opened in 1880 and it was also used to house the fire engine for many years.

Local organisations have also taken advantage of the premises, the Market Deeping Literary Institute making it their headquarters from 1848 and using the upper room for reading and games while the parish council has been holding meetings there since December 1894.

TOWN HALL
Alan Oliver.

The main street at Market Deeping contains two historic hostelries, both formerly coaching inns and one of them, the Bull Inn, dates from the 17th century. The arch is a reminder of this bygone age leading to the stables at the rear while the attractive period stone façade now stands in the heart of the newly-designed town centre area. Across the road is the Deeping Stage, formerly the New Inn, which was built by Joseph Mawby in 1803 although the coaching arch has been converted for use as a lounge area.

By 1743, eight stage coaches were passing through the town each day and although Market Deeping was the pick up point on several routes, it never had its own service based in the town. The Express called here as it galloped between London and Barton-on-Humber, as did the Royal Mail coach while The Perseverance stopped here on its journeys to and from London and Boston and Jackson's stage coach went through the town on its daily runs between Boston and Stamford. In fact, the sight of coaches coming and going caused such wonderment to local people in the 18th century that a tale persists of an old man standing at the crossroads, after a few pints of beer, becoming so excited by the frequent arrivals and departures that he exclaimed: *"Market Deeping, the hub of the universe."*

There was great competition between the two inns as they vied for the passing trade with their advertisements offering good food and well-aired beds. In 1825 the landlord of the New Inn, Oliver Speight, proclaimed that nobility, gentry and commercial friends had conferred their distinguished patronage on him and that his unremitting attention to their comfort and accommodation would merit a continuance of their favour and support. Thomas Dawson of the Bull Inn retaliated by promising gentlemen and travellers everywhere accommodation with wines and post chaises and also begged leave to add that he had stabling for one hundred horses and was capable of furnishing any number of post horses for gentlemen's carriages that may be required.

MARKET DEEPING

THE BULL
EVERARDS
Alan Oliver

The beauty of Deeping St. James is its riverside location, the River Welland running for much of its length alongside the straggle of cottages and houses, many picturesque and all worthy of close inspection for the curious because they are a reflection of the village of yesteryear. Some are small and thatched, such as Clematis Cottage, while others are grandly built of stone with modern brick residences dotted in between blending ancient and modern.

The older properties are redolent of times past, occasionally giving up their secrets, and during rebuilding work in 1973, one cottage was found to be 500 years old when a pile of documents placed in the roof by a former owner in 1846 were discovered detailing its past history as a public house known as The Indian Queen. Another public house overlooking the river which survives to this day, the Crown and Anchor, is unique in that it was run by the Penney family for almost a hundred years. Interesting finds have also been discovered in the river, notably a rare Bellarmine jug which was brought up while the waterway was being cleaned. This glazed brown stoneware receptacle, dating from the 17th century, was in good condition and decorated with a grotesque face and a Germanic coat of arms.

There is a road on one side and a footpath on the other, although there was some concern about the safety of the path during the 19th century after John Robert Lambert accidentally fell into the water and drowned. The *Stamford Mercury* subsequently reported on Friday 12th March 1875:

> *'As further proof of the necessity for an immediate improvement in this locality, it is said that one man who has resided near the river there for many years has rescued eleven persons who have fallen in.'*

The footpath is now greatly improved and is quite safe, becoming one of the most pleasant walks in the district, especially on a sunny day, taking in a mix of properties with differing architectural styles and a quaint crossing with a picturesque warning sign erected by villagers to safeguard ducks from passing traffic.

Bridge Street

DEEPING ST. JAMES

Alan Oliver

The River Welland has been used since ancient times by merchants, travellers, monks and pilgrims, their flat-bottomed craft carrying coal, grain, wool and wine and may even have been used to transport the famous Barnack rag stone from the quarries near Stamford for the churches and manor houses that sprang up over the centuries.

The High Locks at Deeping St. James provide a picturesque setting today but were originally installed to increase trade. The first lock was built of timber with a wooden footbridge for pedestrians and was in constant use by barges transporting goods between Spalding and Stamford upstream, drawn by either one or two horses using the adjoining towpath.

The barges, capable of carrying up to twenty tons, were guided into the lock pen and the gates closed to allow the water level to rise to that in the upper part of the river. The craft would then glide out bound for the wharves at Market Deeping and on to Stamford with several more similar locks to negotiate before the journey ended with the same routine for the return trip. The coming of the railways during the mid-19th century robbed the waterway of its cargo trade, leaving the locks to deteriorate and soon there were complaints that the old wooden railings and footbridge had become so unsafe that villagers preferred to use the pack horse bridge downstream.

A new iron structure was built in 1905 and strengthened in 1949 because it was showing signs of wear. The structure is now maintained as a popular public amenity but has required constant attention because of deterioration through rusting. The river at this point was also greatly altered after the great floods which inundated the fens in 1947 and the waterway has since been narrowed and deepened and the banks strengthened with stonework and riverside railings.

Over the years, the High Locks have become an attraction for anglers who fish in the lock pools below while the river at this point has gained a reputation as a beauty spot, attracting many visitors and Sunday afternoon walkers.

The High Locks

DEEPING ST. JAMES

Alan Oliver.

One of the curiosities of Deeping St. James is the ancient stone lockup that can be found in the main street. Once a place of incarceration for wrongdoers and now a tourist attraction, it was originally the market cross dating from the reign of Edward III in the 14th century. In 1819, it was converted for use as the village round house or lockup, the work being carried out by a local craftsman, Tailby Johnson, at a cost of nine shillings. The interior is five feet square and contains three stone alcoves for seats that were fitted with manacles and chains to secure felons who were ordered to be incarcerated there.

The lockup was one of many tiny houses of correction that began to appear throughout the country in the late 18th century, purpose-built prisons where drunks, vagrants and other petty offenders were locked up overnight before appearing before the magistrates next morning. They were sometimes known as guard houses or round houses but all were 'blind' houses because they had no windows, only grilles high in the walls or set in the doors for ventilation as here at Deeping.

There were also many local names for them, often derogatory, including the blind house or cooler, terms that persist today in connection with over-indulgence in alcohol. Blind drunk, for instance, was a description for any suitable candidate for the blind house and hotheads liable to cause trouble faced the prospect of a spell in the lockup where they could cool down. Tales are still told in many villages that have a lockup of temporary inmates being supplied with liquor and pipes of tobacco by relatives.

The Deeping lockup was cleaned and restored in 1999 at a cost of almost £20,000, money provided by South Kesteven District Council, local charities and various grants, which was well spent because it not only ensured the survival of an historic curiosity but is also a reminder that we live in more forgiving times.

The Lockup

DEEPING ST. JAMES

Alan Oliver.

The date on the stonework of the pack horse bridge at Deeping St. James is 1651 and it was built in an age when transport was far slower and usually horse-drawn, both on and off the river. The three segmental arches are all nearly semi-circular in shape and the bridge carries a roadway only 13 feet wide but there are recesses or alcoves where, as the name implies, mules loaded with goods could wait to enable carts and carriages pass by.

The bridge links the village with Deeping Gate and the main A15 Peterborough to Lincoln road and is still in use by modern traffic and, although there is insufficient room for two cars to pass, it carries an increasing number of vehicles each day which has necessitated strengthening the stonework in recent years although a weight restriction now operates to protect it from damage by heavy vans and lorries.

Nearby, the Bell Inn stands at the very foot of the bridge. Formerly known as the Blue Bell Hotel, it served the community for many purposes in past times including regular meetings of many organisations such as the local angling club in the large clubroom on the upper floor as well as wedding receptions and even property auctions. There was a spell in the late 20th century when the exterior of the building raised eyebrows after being painted a shocking pink, a colour considered to be incongruous in a farming community, but it has since reverted to its familiar cream.

This stretch of the River Welland was also a popular spot for fishing and especially boating, a leisurely pastime during Edwardian times when even ladies could be found on the water in craft that could be hired locally while the annual Sprit Boat was a competitive event in which entrants would propel their flat bottomed fishing punts down river from the High Locks to the bridge, the race taking its name from the sprit or long wooden pole shod with a brass or iron tip which was plunged into the river bed and then energetically pushed on to provide the power.

The Bridge

DEEPING ST. JAMES

Alan Oliver

Water mills have been a feature of the great corn growing regions such as Lincolnshire for more than a thousand years. Some were sited on the larger waterways and their tributaries and others on small streams that have virtually dried up today. Along the western edges of the fens there are several that have survived on the main rivers such as the Welland although none of them is today using water power to grind corn and most have been converted for other uses, usually residential.

The *Domesday Book,* the great land survey ordered by William the Conqueror in 1086, records that there were four water mills at West Deeping but this probably included the mills at nearby Lolham and Maxey. One of them, West Deeping Mill, stands at the south end of the village close to St. Andrew's Church, beautifully restored as a family home during the late 20th century and a surprise around the bend as you approach.

The mill suffered severe damage by fire which broke out in the early hours of the morning in May 1856 when two employees lost their lives. Neighbours who tried to save them were driven back by the intense heat and the bodies of the victims were recovered next morning from the mill stream after it had been drained. A fire engine was despatched from Deeping St. James to tackle the blaze and some items of furniture were salvaged but money and account books were destroyed together with large quantities of corn and flour. Several valuable items were also recovered from the water, a silver watch belonging to one of the dead men and some silver spoons but a quantity of gold and silver plate also thought to be in the water was never found. The mill was subsequently rebuilt after the disaster and resumed its normal role of grinding corn for the next 100 years.

Molecey Mill also survives on the south side of the main A16 road between Stamford and Market Deeping, an imposing building set within its own grounds also on the banks of the River Welland with a date stone inscribed 1773.

The Old Water Mill

WEST DEEPING

Alan Oliver

If you want to find out more about this beautiful area the following may be of interest to you.

Birkbeck, J. D., *A History of Bourne,* 1970 & 1976
Chamberlin, Russell, *English Market Towns,* 1985
Day, F. A., *History of the Deepings*
Hall, Virginia Diane, *A Portrait of West Deeping,* 1995
Lambert, Tim, *A Brief History of Stamford*
Lloyd, Michael, *Portrait of Lincolnshire,* 1983
Needle, Rex, *A Portrait of Bourne* on CD-ROM, 1998-2009
Needle, Rex, *Tales of Bourne from Past Times,* 2009
Pevsner, Nikolaus and John Harris, *The Buildings of England – Lincolnshire,* 1964
Rawnsley, William Franklin, *Highways and Byways in Lincolnshire,* 1914
Roffe, David, *A History of Stamford Castle,* 2002
Simpson, Keith, *A History of the Market Deeping Essential Oil Distillery,* 2008
Stamford – The Official Guide edited by Stamford Town Council
Smith, Martin, *History of Stamford*
Thorold, Henry, *Lincolnshire Churches Revisited,* 1989

Deepings Heritage, *A Glimpse of the Past – Deeping St. James,* 1998
Deeping St. James Family and Local History Group, *From Bridge to Boundary* 2003
Bourne in Words and Pictures: www.bourne-lincs.org.uk
Grimsthorpe Castle Park & Gardens: www.grimsthorpe.co.uk

This title is one in a new series
by **Cottage Publications**.
For more information and to see our other
titles, please visit our website
www.cottage-publications.com
or alternatively you can contact us as follows:–
Telephone: +44 (0)28 9188 8033
Fax: +44 (0)28 9188 8063

Cottage Publications
is an imprint of
Laurel Cottage Ltd.,
15 Ballyhay Road,
Donaghadee, Co. Down,
N. Ireland, BT21 0NG